IN THE
NATIONAL INTEREST

General Sir John Monash once exhorted a graduating class to 'equip yourself for life, not solely for your own benefit but for the benefit of the whole community'. At the university established in his name, we repeat this statement to our own graduating classes, to acknowledge how important it is that common or public good flows from education.

Universities spread and build on the knowledge they acquire through scholarship in many ways, well beyond the transmission of this learning through their education. It is a necessary part of a university's role to debate its findings, not only with other researchers and scholars, but also with the broader community in which it resides.

Publishing for the benefit of society is an important part of a university's commitment to free intellectual inquiry. A university provides civil space for such inquiry by its scholars, as well as for investigations by public intellectuals and expert practitioners.

This series, In the National Interest, embodies Monash University's mission to extend knowledge and encourage informed debate about matters of great significance to Australia's future.

Professor Margaret Gardner AC
President and Vice-Chancellor,
Monash University

SCOTT RYAN

CHALLENGING POLITICS

MONASH
UNIVERSITY
PUBLISHING

Monash University Publishing
Matheson Library Annexe
40 Exhibition Walk
Monash University
Clayton, Victoria 3800, Australia
https://publishing.monash.edu

Monash University Publishing brings to the world publications which advance the best traditions of humane and enlightened thought.

ISBN: 9781922464279 (paperback)
ISBN: 9781922464293 (ebook)

Series: In the National Interest
Editor: Louise Adler
Project manager & copyeditor: Paul Smitz
Designer: Peter Long
Typesetter: Cannon Typesetting
Proofreader: Gillian Armitage
Printed in Australia by Ligare Book Printers

A catalogue record for this book is available from the National Library of Australia.

The paper this book is printed on is in accordance with the standards of the Forest Stewardship Council®. The FSC® promotes environmentally responsible, socially beneficial and economically viable management of the world's forests.

For Nick and Ben.

May the open minds and optimism of youth
always be strong in our politics.

PREFACE

When I was first elected to the Senate for Victoria in 2007, Australia had long been experiencing remarkably stable and predictable government, having changed governments at elections only six times since the end of World War II, and usually by convincing majorities. Political debates were contested in mass-circulation newspapers and broadcast media shared by the overwhelming majority of the population. Compulsory voting— then as now—ensured mass participation in elections, and that political parties needed to compete for the concerns of voters who did not see themselves as tied to a particular entity. The parties themselves were the most significant institutions in political debate, and their ideas and policies dominated those put forward for electoral consideration.

The years since 2007 have been particularly challenging, with Australia experiencing a period of political unpredictability at the national level. The 2010 election produced the first hung parliament and minority government since 1940. Both the 2016 and 2019 elections produced the narrowest possible electoral margins in over half a century, since the single-seat victory of the Coalition in 1961. The fractures within parties widened and contributed to leadership instability. It has been the most tumultuous period for politics since the late 1960s to the mid-1970s.

Simply put, the environment in which politics, elections and government operate has recently undergone significant change, and previous assumptions about the stability of government, the way to deal with conflicting priorities, and the competing pressures on those making decisions, no longer apply. In particular, the pattern of constant and predictable economic growth was challenged first by the global financial crisis (GFC) of 2007–08, and a decade later by the COVID 19 pandemic. This has been reflected both in personal and household perspectives on economic wellbeing and in the revenue available to government to address public priorities.

Another significant factor has been the media, which is the currency of politics. The relationship between politicians and those who seek to influence them changed profoundly when the internet became ubiquitous on mobile phones. The explosion in digital media, and especially social media, may have given a voice to those who were previously denied one by the mass media, but it has also ensured that citizens don't share the same information, experiences and understanding that they once did. Many now spend a good deal of their time exchanging views only with those who have the same interests, sentiments, priorities and even prejudices as themselves.

Why does this matter? Because the key function of politics is to make decisions that are in the common interest in a collective manner, through the institution of parliament. We go about this via elections that determine the formation of governments and the make-up of parliaments, with the aim of ensuring accountability and legitimacy in regard to the deliberation and endorsement of policy initiatives. And for these debates to be conducted requires some element of shared, common knowledge.

Australia has been a remarkably successful democracy, imperfect like all, but with the capacity to evolve and deal with emerging issues—or issues, such as in the case of the treatment of our Indigenous people, that we have failed to consider appropriately for much of our history as a nation. At its core, democracy requires the ability to deliberate, discuss and occasionally compromise. It is this process, undertaken through elections and parliamentary consideration, that delivers legitimacy and the acceptance of policies and priorities that parts of the community inevitably disagree with.

As the apex of our political system, our parliament is where this happens. For decades now, this has primarily been expressed by the formation of government through the House of Representatives, with the Senate, which is elected differently, providing the forum for deliberation, negotiation and compromise. The Senate is the catalyst for compromise: it institutionalises its importance. Challenging and contentious issues, from the introduction of the goods and services tax (GST) to the resolution of native title following the High Court ruling in Mabo, have been explored and resolved through this process.

As a senator, one is closer to all this simply by virtue of the chamber itself and the work it undertakes. Lacking a government majority, as is usually the case in the House of Representatives, whether as a backbencher, minister or presiding officer, much more time is spent with colleagues across other parties exploring, debating, discussing and even negotiating everything from the operation of the chamber to the fate of legislation. The committees of the Senate ensure that senators spend a considerable amount of time with one another dealing with contentious issues. It is the moments of conflict that grab the headlines, but it's the hundreds of hours spent with one another without public conflict that allow you to better understand the multitude of different perspectives that exist.

This isn't to dismiss the role of politicians in vigorously pursuing an agenda. All of us who seek to enter public life do so with our own values and priorities in mind. I came into politics with passions of my own a dozen years ago. But one of the realities of being a newly elected member of parliament is that you quickly learn how politics is about lots of people having their own priorities, even within parties, and that you have to negotiate and, yes, even compromise on this enormous spectrum of views in order to achieve anything.

A party's policy program never reflects an individual's goals but rather the shared priorities and compromises of the party's members. It also reflects a process of internal deliberation, albeit not one that happens under the glare of the parliamentary spotlight. As a member of parliament, even as a minister, there are constraints on your actions and preferences, and it is a threshold requirement to generate consent for one's policy preferences, starting from within and then with the broader public.

Elections, after all, are a means of resolving the issue of which competing set of priorities and which values are reflected in government. But politics, and parliaments, are not merely a platform for an electoral victor. They also provide a guaranteed forum for thrashing out competing views. Political leadership cannot fully function without the ability to pursue an agenda *and* negotiate unforeseen circumstances, compromising with others to address these before moving on to the next matter. The defining nature of a political party, as opposed to a political movement, is standing candidates for election, with a specific program for which you are seeking public endorsement.

And what of the economic and social changes we have witnessed over the last decade? These have changed the environment in which this whole process occurs, and our political institutions must continually evolve in order to meet that challenge.

Compromise doesn't mean everyone agrees, nor does it mean the lowest common denominator prevails. It can mean deciding how to amend or limit the dominant perspective so that alternative views are incorporated. It can mean allowing the process of deliberation and debate to play an important part in generating consent to the final outcome, or at least in convincing a minority that the outcome reflects the views of a larger proportion of fellow citizens. It also means acknowledging the truism that there are few simple, straightforward solutions to any policy challenge. Importantly, it ensures that those involved better understand the perspectives of people with different views and experiences, which usually leads to better and less-contested decisions and outcomes.

The concept of compromise—and associated elements such as deliberation and negotiation—is critical to governing. Some bemoan it as not reflecting 'the base', or as a cynically pragmatic stance. However, the alternative is not politics as we might wish for, in the sense of stability and conflict resolution. It is politics in the sense of tribes merely competing to utilise the power of the state for their own preferences, absent the consideration of minority views, and with a consequent lack of public consent and acquiescence that will spark further political conflict.

In this book, I will not be arguing that strongly held views should be put aside, or that there is no place in our system for firm political leadership, or that one should always compromise whenever resistance is encountered. Leadership on an issue can bring it before the public for consideration, place it on the parliamentary agenda, and result in change. Indeed, some major achievements, such as Medicare and firm border protection measures, were predominantly the result of one side's electoral victory. And if these are followed by clear, repeated expressions of public affirmation, a form of bipartisan acceptance emerges: the Coalition came to support Medicare after early opposition, and the Labor Party now claims to strongly support the Coalition's border-protection policies. But implementing policy, actually putting it into effect, can require compromise.

Nor do I argue that progress is only possible by compromise. Attempts have been made to resolve important issues, for example, by governments working with minor parties to create a new status quo that comes to be accepted. Paul Keating did so with the Democrats in regard to native title following the Mabo decision, with the Coalition then amending the legislation with the support of independent senators after the Wik decision. The Coalition also entrenched the GST through its work with the Democrats.

I still retain the views that drove me into politics: support for free trade, freer markets and lower taxes; balancing budgets so as not to run up debt for future generations; reducing rather than expanding restrictions on speech and publication; and deregulating labour markets. But I don't suggest that my personal views are those of the average voter. Politics isn't simply about doing what I desire as a politician. It's primarily about dealing with what the public prioritises while applying the values I hold, as well as dealing with unforeseen circumstances—or, in the (likely apocryphal) words of former British prime minister Harold Macmillan, 'Events, dear boy, events.'

Politics has always been difficult. After all, it involves dealing with the aspirations and needs of the millions of our fellow citizens, not to mention their diverse views on how this should be done. This has always required practical compromise—not just to reach a settlement on a given issue, but to be able to move on to the myriad other issues waiting to be addressed. I contend that it is this element of politics that is getting more difficult, and that if we do not understand why this is so and what we might do about it, we will all be disappointed, no matter our world view.

An essential piece of our political system is in trouble, and if we don't find a way to re-enliven it, we will face deepening political gridlock—a fixation on a small set of issues that motivate activists and others passionate about them above others, at the cost of government addressing the much wider range of issues prioritised across the Australian community.

The art of compromise helps us to agree on solutions, even if they are imperfect. It frees us to deal with the inevitable next issue—and there are always more issues to deal with. And it relies on dialogue and persuasion, rather than warring tribes yelling at each other. To enable real social and economic advancement, politics can't just be war by other means. It must be the resolution of conflict by all possible means.

CHALLENGING POLITICS

Recent years have seen electoral results and other political developments that have particularly surprised those who consider themselves well informed—indeed, those who consider themselves expert, from practitioners such as politicians to direct close observers such as the mainstream media and academia. Examples across democracies Australians are familiar with include the success of the Brexit referendum in the United Kingdom, the election of Donald Trump in the United States, the rise then return to earth of Emmanuel Macron and En Marche!

in France, and the eclipse of longstanding parties across Europe.

But how much of this should really surprise us? So many experts experienced disbelief and shock in the wake of these developments, yet there is a rational explanation for all of this.

The word 'populism' is often used to describe this trend, but it's a term I've always been uncomfortable with. Democracies are supposed to consider popular support and consent as a yardstick, so using it in a derogatory fashion is counterintuitive. Rather, I contend that the key elements that should concern us are the attacks on politics itself and the dismissal of complexity in addressing various policy challenges, as if there are simple, easy solutions that are being ignored by a conspiracy of those in power. When the motives of those involved in politics are impugned, as a substitute for focusing on the impact of specific policies or proposals, it is not political debate that is occurring but a drive towards political tribalism that is intentionally encouraging one group to not even listen to the alternative views or perspectives of others. These are the very factors making domestic politics 'harder' than it used to be, leading to frustration from those claiming to be directly engaged, and disengagement and disillusionment from the wider population.

Alongside the unexpected electoral outcomes, there has also been a rise in political conflict regarding issues that are either binary in nature (such as the Brexit referendum) or where movements challenge the core institutions of politics without specific policy demands that can be implemented to address the relevant concerns.

For example, in the United States, a key difference between the modern Black Lives Matter (BLM) movement and the civil rights movement of the 1950s and 1960s is the generality of the demands of BLM. Whereas the push for civil rights included calls for the repeal or override of the Jim Crow segregation laws that condemned African Americans to second-class citizenship, the generality of the BLM claims makes them more difficult to actually address.

Without specific claims, it is obviously much more difficult to address aspirations and concerns. In particular, this reflects how the movement itself may not have determined the policy priorities that it believes will help it achieve its desired outcome.

Politics requires specificity. That is how public resources are allocated. It is how success is measured. The common experience of a grievance, no matter how valid, is impossible to address without some agreement on a course of action to resolve it.

Furthermore, the world in which all this has occurred has arguably changed more in the last decade than at any other time since television became commonplace in the 1950s. But unlike during the expansion of mass media, we have separated. We're all spending more time talking and listening to people like ourselves, those who hold similar views of the world and its problems and the causes of these, those with whom we share similar social and economic experiences and life-styles. There are now larger groups of people who disagree on fundamental challenges like climate change. So it really shouldn't be a surprise that groups which are becoming more insular along these lines are collectively shocked when their expectations are overturned.

That the modern, fragmented media world leads people to spend more time talking to those who see things just as they do, rather than those who see things differently, is not a new insight. But we may have underestimated just how widespread has been the impact on politics. This is not about something as simple as different media 'noise' but a development that is changing the incentives and rewards in politics, and there-fore the behaviour of all those involved.

Most of all, this is about us as citizens. As a democracy, our behaviour influences how politicians behave as they seek our support, whether as part of single-issue groups or broader political movements.

THE CHANGING MEDIA WORLD

Decades ago, the American historian Bernard Bailyn outlined the impact of 'pamphlets' on the American Revolution. Early printed 'newspapers'—not much more than handbills or leaflets, passed by hand in public houses, churches, shops and marketplaces—were critical in creating the environment for many otherwise conservative churchgoing farmers and traders to rise up against the British Empire. This culture continued in the politics of the new republic, before the rise of the mass media. Some of these pamphlets were scandalous, containing outrageous personal abuse and extraordinary allegations about political opponents' personal lives and policies. Eventually, they evolved into highly partisan newspapers with wide circulations.

People at that time often received news based on the perspective it represented, just like the stories they heard and the sermons they attended within communities comprising citizens of similar views and outlook. The mandates of geography and communication created communities of shared experience.

Now replace the old technologies of handbills and the printing press with global connectivity and you have the modern world of digital and social media, with news no longer bound by location. People still seek, receive and believe information from sources they have come to know and trust, but often with little in the way of verification or fact checking, as is a norm of traditional journalism, and with algorithms and online communities replacing the community of church or town selecting what is heard, seen and read. And, of course, there are the slurs and claims of personal abuse.

The effect is the same, but amplified by the speed and capability of modern technology: a rise in personal and personality-driven comments and attacks; claims striving for an emotional response; and disputes over basic facts that previously would have been accepted, leading to a dramatic increase in the spread of disinformation.

This reversion to an older world of media, albeit with new systems, has occurred mainly due to technology breaking down the critical intermediating role once played by the mass media, that which arose with increasing literacy and broad-circulation newspapers, and which further evolved via radio and television in the twentieth century.

In future years, we may view the twentieth-century world of a common, shared mass media as the exception rather than the rule. Our fragmented 21st-century media and information environment better reflects the experiences of the eighteenth and nineteenth centuries. Despite technology making it appear an evolution, it is actually a reversion.

THE IMPACT OF MEDIA ON POLITICS

What does all this mean for politics? Well, media isn't everything, but it undoubtedly directly influences the behaviour of political actors— politicians, the media, interest groups—and especially the attitudes, reactions and expectations of citizens. Communication is the currency and lifeblood of politics.

It was less than two decades ago that most politicians rarely ventured in front of a television camera. TV exposure was for senior figures in the government and the Opposition; even many ministers rarely appeared on the small screen. The advent of 24-hour channels such as Sky News and ABC News changed all that, with virtually all federal MPs having access to a media platform they previously had been denied. The same is true for industry associations, lobbyists, think tanks and others seeking to promote a view or policy.

Compounding this is the rise of 'opinion-news', which is expressed through networks such as Fox News and MSNBC in the United States and the evening schedule of Sky News in Australia. Not only does this seek out a specific opinionated audience, but it attempts to further encourage a particular perspective on issues in the daily news. Political debates have become an arena in which to pick and follow a side, rather than follow issues. Sky News at night has become Fox Footy for those who see politics as tribal. Social media, meanwhile, provides yet another outlet.

The mass media feeds on and supercharges contentious statements that arise in these fora, thereby providing an incentive for participants to be ever more antagonistic.

The upshot is that those who seek to influence public debate, including political candidates themselves, can now go directly to the voters and distinct communities in much more targeted ways, often without the verification process inherent in the traditional media. This in turn opens up much wider opportunities for campaigns aimed at grievances, or even for simple lies or mistruths to be spread and gain traction, in a way that just wasn't possible when mass media was shared. That's because what citizens see, read and hear impacts not just their perceptions of political figures—especially leaders—but also of issues, with the unavoidable consequence that this affects voters' attitudes towards policy priorities and those who implement them.

In a democracy, politicians can occasionally lead, but the expectations and reactions of voters inevitably determine the path of politics in the long run. This isn't to dismiss the importance of challenging the status quo, or arguing for a change in public attitudes—politics can never simply be about following public opinion. But in a democracy, for those in office, there is always a balance to be sought between addressing public priorities and promoting one's own.

The media as a key institution is under unique commercial pressure, but also a competitive pressure as audiences turn elsewhere. What is the role of the traditional media when their audiences are abandoning them? In particular, the consumption of traditional mass media has a distinct demographic trend: younger Australians don't read a newspaper, listen to news radio or watch the evening news in the way that once—only a generation ago—defined politics and drove the rise and fall of governments.

Two decades ago, John Howard's use of talkback radio was perceived as a key ability in directly communicating with masses of voters, and while bypassing part of the filter of the media, it was also rebroadcast across radio and television and covered in newspapers. And in the 1980s, sales of newspapers in a Melbourne half its current size were a million or so daily, with community-wide penetration. The intermediating role of the media comprised the selection of issues that received coverage and the voices put forward. Through this control, a common set of facts was shared, and to a lesser extent a common frame through which to view electoral contests and debates that directly affected everyone. But in the run-up to the November 2018 Victorian election, the avoidance of traditional mass news media by Daniel Andrews and the preferencing of social media not subject to any effective scrutiny via wider coverage was considered a key element of his political success.

These trends all mean that the common, shared information once provided by the media is simply not present in the way it used to be. And as negotiation and compromise require both an understanding of the perspectives of others and a common set of facts, this disaggregation makes for more voices but arguably fewer shared facts and less common experience.

The impact of complex policy proposals like taxation illustrates this. The GST tax reform debates of 1998 focused on the notion of 'fairness' around common facts, such as the impact of the changes on various households. But since then, we have seen taxation debates less focused on such common facts, with the most recent regarding the effects of dividend imputation and refunds for retirees at least as much focused on disagreements about their impact.

NO WINNERS WITHOUT LOSERS

One of the core activities of politics is public resource allocation; that is, determining how to spend the funds collected by government through taxation, and the level and burden of this taxation. This reflects the policy priorities, but it also determines the balance and distribution of costs and benefits, whether directly and immediately through taxation, deferred through debt, or involving the imposition of regulatory measures that distribute costs such as tariffs. The concept of a trade-off here is essential and intrinsic. It means that more spending on one priority means less spending somewhere else, or a combination of more spending and debt or higher taxes. It can mean that the protection or preferment of an industry without a direct subsidy must come through distributed costs imposed upon others, such as via trade barriers or tariffs.

Every single decision of government therefore involves a process of prioritisation to address some of the effectively endless series of claims on public resources. And this direction or allocation of resources will always disappoint some claimant. Consequently, one of the key functions of democratic elections is to determine which set of trade-offs the electorate prefers.

But especially in Australia, and particularly over the second part of the country's long boom since the early 2000s, the political contest has often been absent explicit consideration of this inevitable trade-off, in that the costs to be imposed are not completely apparent, or have been hidden. Up until recently, growing government revenues have meant that new policies could be initiated without explicit tax increases—the burden of bracket creep is not one that all voters feel in the same way. And so the spending on central public services such as old age pensions, health and education continued to grow without sacrifices being made in other areas of government expenditure.

While sometimes crudely described in electoral terms as the 'hip pocket nerve', this reflected the priorities of both the electorate, as expressed via elections, and those elected to govern. As a country that hadn't faced an existential threat in generations, our politics were largely about appeals to winners, without any direct 'cost' to a political loser.

Political stress can be acute when public expectations of politics suddenly change. While the GFC crystallised this change in many parts of the democratic world, notably in Europe, it was only very recently that the ability of Australian politics to consistently provide electoral incentives through the targeted allocation of public funds or resources without 'losers' has come unstuck. 'Austerity', for instance, never became a major term in the Australian conversation about the GFC like it did in the United Kingdom, where it effectively defined the David Cameron/Nick Clegg coalition government of Conservatives and Liberal Democrats—although the stated aspiration of both major parties to balance the budget, if not specifically repay debt, eventually ran into the fiscal reality. Regardless, if there was any doubt about all this in Australia, it vanished when we were hit with COVID-19, which has had an unforeseen and unprecedented impact on the lives of millions of people here.

Certainly, even past debates have depended on compromise for their resolution. Economic resources, for example, have often been used to generate consent for otherwise difficult public policies. The implementation of the GST by the Howard government was accompanied by tax cuts and increases in various payments, in an attempt to ensure people subsequently would not be worse off, and to generate political consent for the policy along with the first sustained period of real wage growth in many years. In the 1980s, the introduction of the 'social wage' by the Hawke government, most prominently Medicare, was used to generate consent for the wage containment policy under the Prices and Income Accord with the Australian Council of Trade Unions.

However, the truth is that when issues of economics and finance are at the centre of public debate, in some ways compromise is easier as the terms can be negotiated. More compensation can be offered to those concerned about costs because funding is flexible and fungible. But in an environment where the role of the media has changed, as outlined above, debates over complex policies that involve substantial changes in how resources are allocated, and to whom, become substantially more difficult. Climate change policy, Kevin Rudd's Carbon Pollution Reduction Scheme, Julia Gillard and Bob Brown's 'carbon tax', the original Resource Super Profits Tax or similar redesigned mining taxes, the 2019 election campaign on extra social spending funded by specific taxes—all those discussions were dominated to various degrees by who the losers were, the extent of the costs imposed versus the opportunities the new revenues offered, and the impact on various sections of the economy and community.

This was a new development compared with the 2000s, when political patronage, preferment, and new policies and promises funded from substantially increased revenues didn't come with easily identified or defined political losers. The fact is that the days of predictable increases in revenues are behind us. The resources available to government are constrained, both economically and politically, and greater spending has to be funded.

If anything, the coronavirus pandemic brought this into sharper relief. While there was broad acceptance of the need for a sharp increase in spending predicated on previously unacceptable levels of public borrowing and debt, there continued to be a debate about the extent of the spending, the form it would take, and to whom it was to be directed. Should it be short and sharp to address the immediate effects of the downturn, or should it be used to permanently reshape the size and role of government and the funding of public services in the wider economy? But the economic reality could not be denied, regardless of one's view of the role of government or the impact of stimulus. It is a reality that will constrain the choices of future generations, and therefore the future resources available to the political process to 'buy' compromise when policies are contested.

HISTORICALLY UTILITARIAN, BUT CHANGING

In 1985, in a long piece for the journal *Daedalus* titled 'Political Ideology in Australia', Hugh Collins wrote of Australia as a Benthamite political society. He described Australian political culture as one that values utilitarianism, or a practical focus on achieving the greatest good for the greatest number of people—and specifically, a focus that placed this practical consideration above ideological contests. Summarising this, he wrote: 'Political institutions and policies are to be assessed in terms of the impact of their operation upon the interests of the majority ... the sum of individual interests.' Not for Australia the moralistic tone of American politics, putting everything in terms of right or wrong. We prefer to concentrate on the practical impact of policy and politics.

Our history is littered with examples of political parties and movements that have failed by becoming captive to the interests and priorities of their own active and passionate members. Such groups have been prone to risking electoral defeat by advocating for what might be unkindly labelled crusades or pet projects considered to lie a step too far from the practical centre of politics. The danger has been especially acute where alternatives voices are not heeded—or that is seen to be the case—or where negotiations do not sufficiently take into account those who do not share the same priorities.

The government of Stanley Bruce lost the surprise 1929 election partly due to its attempts to overturn the widely supported policy of wage arbitration. The government of Ben Chifley lost power in 1949 partly because of its commitment to maintaining certain World War II economic controls and failed attempts at nationalisation. In 1996, Paul Keating was perceived to be focusing on native title and engagement with the region—think the now-forgotten security pact with Indonesia—at the expense of more mundane domestic economic matters. In 2007, Work Choices was a major catalyst for the defeat of John Howard. While there is rarely a single reason for an electoral loss, these examples represent parties pushing ideological preferences beyond the public's tolerance.

Sometimes, the electoral consequences can be startling; for example, the defeat in 2015 of Queensland premier Campbell Newman, only three years after gaining an unprecedented electoral majority, and Jeff Kennett's loss in 1999 in a Victorian election he was expected to win at a canter. Nonetheless, the common thread is the perception of government having become too 'ideological' and refusing to heed warnings about public discontent.

The only test consistently applied to policy development in Australia that has what could be described as a moral element is that of 'fairness'. Any politician thought to cross this line places themselves on an electoral precipice. But as well as being disposed to discussion in utilitarian terms—for example, asking how many people benefit from a policy, and to what extent or by how much—it is also a malleable test, one that can be subject to the political environment and context. The time-limited test and work require-ments for access to unemployment benefits proposed by John Hewson in 1993, when unemployment stood at around one million people, were regarded as unfair. Yet the strict 'mutual obligation' requirements and work for the dole initiative for younger Australians introduced by the Howard government, in an era of low and falling unemployment, did pass the fairness test; indeed, the Coalition government claimed 'fairness' as one of its attributes.

A reasonable conclusion here is that even the practical fairness test can be passed by negotiation and compromise. And yet the new world described above is challenging this assumption.

A LACK OF NUANCE

One key issue is that the tone and terms of debate have changed, particularly in the world of a disaggregated and social media. Mass media historically sought to report rather than opine, even if the way in which news was selected inevitably had an impact in determining those issues in the public's mind. But now, with mass media lacking the penetration and exclusivity it once had, the new media is not so constrained. The blurry distinction between reportage and commentary, and the myriad voices all claiming different impacts for a specific policy, make it much more difficult to deliberate using common facts, and it is now less likely that a common mindset will emerge.

For example, the debates about the cost of renewable energy subsidies and the targets undertaken by state/territory and federal governments often runs into the much simpler question of whether these will ultimately increase or decrease the price of electricity to consumers. It is almost impossible to decide whether such costs are worthwhile when we cannot agree on whether they exist at all.

Looking at social media, you can see a reflection of the age of pamphleteering, when shamelessly and emotively taking one side in a debate, pushing a particular opinion, was rife. Even in the less-partisan sections of the new media, the shorter format itself increasingly describes in moral tones issues previously discussed in predominantly utilitarian terms. Tax cuts for corporations are no longer just ineffective or unfair but are talked about in terms of whether they are wrong in principle. Even a highly complex issue like climate change is framed in moral terms—Kevin Rudd once described it as the 'great moral challenge of our time'.

When complex issues are debated emotionally and simplistically, then effective negotiation and decision-making become more difficult. They are often distilled into a binary form in which shades of meaning cannot be acknowledged.

For instance, the resolution in the 1970s of long-term social issues such as the decriminalisation of homosexuality and abortion, and ending capital punishment, meant a return to the more traditional focus on social policy delivery, such as health, education, the economy and national security. But recent arguments over marriage equality and euthanasia entailed mainly binary responses that were unavoidably framed in moral terms.

Such social issues are not only more suited to the less-complex world of social media, they also arouse deep passions, by their nature reflecting deeply held values that are more difficult to craft a compromise around.

Binary 'legal/illegal' or 'allowed/not allowed' alternatives do not permit nuance. One cannot negotiate a legislative agreement on whether marriage should be limited to a man and a woman or opened up to any couple. And even where it may be possible for some gradation, there are still many who strongly adhere to one of two positions based on unassailable notions of individual autonomy or the sanctity of heterosexual nuptials. The suggested same-sex marriage plebiscite and subsequent survey was an attempt to find a way around this.

Initially, my own approach to this issue was the same as then prime minister Tony Abbott. I strongly opposed the federal parliament delegating its clear responsibility to consider the issue in a traditional legislative manner. This position was reversed when the Coalition adopted a binding policy to oppose legislative consideration prior to a plebiscite. In my view, this decision weakened the parliament and set a bad precedent for the resolution of contentious social issues. But subsequently, the policy was taken to the 2016 election by Malcolm Turnbull.

The question I then had to ask myself was whether my opinion was of greater importance than the position explicitly taken to, and endorsed at, a federal election by my party. Given the falling level of trust in politicians and in the promises they made, I decided my own view was not the most important one at stake. It was now a matter of following through on a specific electoral commitment.

In the end, the voluntary postal marriage survey was conducted by the Australian Bureau of Statistics—as opposed to a referendum-type plebiscite conducted by the Australian Electoral Commission—and upon its positive result, legislation was passed by parliament to change the *Marriage Act* accordingly. This compromise effectively fulfilled the public promise and delivered a clear outcome. Despite being contentious at the time, this mechanism provided a means of resolving the issue, and public debate was able to move on to other pressing matters. It has to be considered a success in that sense—would the country be better off if we were still debating marriage equality? Compromise requires individuals to accept that their own views cannot always prevail, in this case my own.

IMPUGNING MOTIVES

The changed media landscape and the proliferation of voices has driven a further evolution in the tone of political debate. It is now much more common for motives to be assigned, impugned and attacked than for a conversation to be had about specific measures or outcomes.

In regard to climate change, it is commonly asserted that stronger controls on emissions are avoided because political parties receive donations from fossil fuel mining companies, or because someone is a climate change denier. Or it is said that corporate tax cuts are proposed because big business makes political donations. Or someone who supports the mandatory detention of unlawful arrivals or the policy of turnbacks at sea is accused of doing so because they are racist, or they do not care about the fate of refugees or, more broadly, human life. The list goes on.

This behaviour has become increasingly common in formal debates in parliament and also in the mass media, as well as in much shorter and emotion-driven social media campaigns. Look up the Twitter feed of some minor party politicians and you will see short video grabs of speeches or questions in parliament along these lines.

The consideration that someone might oppose a carbon tax as economically more destructive than environmentally helpful, or that the protection of border integrity is important for maintaining popular support for immigration, is given short shrift by people seeking to impugn the motives of those with whom they disagree. It is then a small step from dismissing the position another holds because of an assumed motive, to personal attacks.

Dismissing a proposal by asserting the illegitimacy of the proposer, or their intentions, is another way in which the fragmentation of political debate is continuing, compounding an already declining level of public trust in politics. It allows the accuser to simply ignore the information or response provided, and to encourage others to do the same. After all, if I think you don't care about climate change as much as I do, then I won't care what your response is—I will see it as an excuse for inaction, rather than as a sincere reason worthy of evaluation. Similarly, if I am led to believe you are a racist, I won't care what reason you give for supporting a particular immigration policy. Thus, political tribes do not engage with one another.

Fuelling this is the same trend we see across the uglier side of social media—personal abuse. We see this in the sewer that short-form social media like Twitter often becomes. Assigning someone a motive, and abusing or insulting them from a distance or anonymously, is at the other end of the spectrum from respectful face-to-face interaction. It shouldn't come as a surprise that this is intensified by people not having to see or meet each other, or that it's a sadly effective way of blocking out alternative world views.

The style of campaign that impugns motives is increasingly coming from single-issue movements and minor parties—critically, those that do not need to govern. These groups are not subject to the requirement to have a coherent policy framework for government, with all of the internal compromises, trade-offs and policy prioritisation that this entails. Indeed, as we shall see, the fact that those who seek to govern actually need to be equipped and prepared to do so becomes weaponised by such groups.

COMPROMISE AS SELLOUT

If the core business of government involves the prioritisation of the resources to be directed to various policy areas, and the time required to do so, then compromise is critical. Every single priority or preference can't be addressed with resources that are always limited; every issue can't be addressed at once, as the effective determination and application of any policy requires the dedicated attention of those undertaking it—initially within political parties in developing an agenda for presentation at election time, but also in the parliamentary process.

Policy represents the values of a political group in terms that can be applied to a challenge.

A commitment to improving public education outcomes, for example, can be expressed through increased funding arrangements, or a redesigned curriculum, or improvements in teacher training. While improved educational outcomes is an aspiration that can be (and is) shared across political parties, the actual means of doing so—the policies and resources directed to it—will be contested. And in delivering on this aspiration, it is the measures themselves that need to be evaluated and firmed through elections and parliament.

As a federation, there is contested power in Australia between the states/territories and the Commonwealth. This occurs particularly with shared areas like education, but in recent times it has been seen in areas traditionally regarded as the sole jurisdiction of one level of government or the other—such as the tension between the Commonwealth and Victoria over the latter's cooperation with China's Belt and

Road Initiative. Across myriad areas of public policy, from water and health to education, infrastructure and economic policy, tension and cooperation between the states/territories and the Commonwealth is a permanent, ongoing feature of Australia. And our political system guarantees that multiple voices are heard not just at elections but between them, in the process of government itself, and at every level.

Any serious Commonwealth policy initiative needs passage of the legislation through the Senate. But over the last four decades, the federal government has only possessed a majority in the Senate for just over two years—from July 2005 until the defeat of the Howard government in November 2007—and this is exceedingly unlikely to happen again in the foreseeable future. These institutional arrangements mean that the government of the day must engage with, and often negotiate with, others—be it state governments or the Opposition or minor parties in the Senate.

Unilateral action is only rarely possible, more so in areas of national security, but far less so when it comes to allocating public resources.

Being open to compromise allows a government to do two things: progress the agenda it has been elected on and thereby validate the election in question; and generate consent for the settlement of those policies by virtue of a wider array of voices being represented in the outcome and thereby partly having a stake in it. It also allows a government to move on to the next public priority, to address the needs of other groups and interests across the community.

However, this capacity has increasingly been challenged in recent years. As politics has become more polarised, some have sought to simply seek attention to capitalise on existing grievances.

When The Greens orchestrated a walkout during the maiden speech of newly elected Senator Pauline Hanson in September 2016, it did so to seek attention, and to make a point to part of the electorate via the subsequent media focus. The alternative of simply not being present for Hanson's first speech, which was entirely open to the party, would not have allowed it to do this. Similarly, when Senator Hanson the following year entered the Senate chamber wearing a burqa, this was entirely directed at catching the eye of the media. Neither of these actions were about addressing an issue. Rather, they were solely about attracting attention and exploiting it for partisan purposes.

The Senate, as the place where minority views are represented, needs to ensure it is not used as a stage for actions that make it *more difficult* to incorporate wider views into government decision-making, or as a forum for expressing narrow perspectives with little intention of addressing issues other than on one's own terms. The more this happens, the more that the act of compromising is then impugned as somehow selling out.

When, in 2015, Labor attacked The Greens for cooperating with the Coalition on pension changes, The Greens attacked Labor for supporting the Coalition's income tax change. Within the Coalition, when Malcolm Turnbull sought to change superannuation taxation arrangements, he was seen as 'attacking the base'. Creating litmus tests for what qualifies as legitimate policy when dealing with complex issues is intended to make the process of deliberation and collaboration more difficult.

The idea that compromise is wrong, that negotiating in order to achieve one objective and thus target another represents a lost political opportunity for a contest or is a 'sellout', is one that weakens those who seek to govern and empowers those who are merely out to take care of their own issues or priorities. Who would think that the country would be better off if John Howard and Peter Costello had not negotiated the successful passage of the GST following the 1998 election?

Or that we would be better off still arguing about it?

Compromise is critical in addressing public priorities, and it must involve complexity and nuance—exactly what is lacking in most social media content, which can be an echo chamber of people's pre-existing prejudices, priorities and attitudes. Ironically, the consequent quest for simplicity in public debate is occurring as we enjoy readier access to greater information than ever before.

THE QUEST FOR SIMPLICITY

The competition for attention among a fragmented commercial media and innumerable personal sources of news drives the use of emotion-laden language (to attract attention) and uncomplicatedness (to make messages suitable for ever-shorter formats). Decades ago, people observed that television had created the ten-second soundbite. Well, that is now a 280-character tweet.

This quest for simplicity in language has morphed into pressure for simplicity in policy. Qualification, distinction and the explanation of risk are increasingly getting lost in the fog caused by the volume of information overwhelming people, and as competitors assert that such nuances imply a less-than-total commitment. This approach understates the complexity of public policy, and it ignores the reality that simple choices rarely guarantee outcomes.

The level of spending on schools and its relationship to educational outcomes is a classic example. Undoubtedly, greater resources can assist in some areas, but not in such a straightforward manner that it is inconsequential to dismiss how and where money is spent. Similarly, the rigour of a curriculum and teacher training matters significantly, albeit not in isolation. Yet debates about school education often fall to claims about the level of government spending, as if that is a reliable measure of the determination to address the issue.

Here, we must differentiate simplicity in communications from that in policy. Expressing and communicating an aspiration in basic terms is not the same as contending there are easy, uncomplicated solutions. 'Stop the boats' represented an aspiration of the Abbott Government and the phrase clearly expresses it, but there was no contention that it would take little effort to do so. Yet in debates over climate change policy, the idea that Australia can rapidly shift from fossil fuel–fired electricity generation to a stable renewable network at little cost, represents the conflation of a simple aspiration—reducing emissions—with the weighty challenges of achieving it.

Many will remember the 'L-A-W, law' tax cuts promised by Paul Keating in his 1993 campaign against the GST. The attempt to make the promise seem so unqualified as to have already passed into law only served to mislead the electorate, as the cuts would be partially repealed almost immediately upon the Keating government's re-election.

John Howard was attacked in 2007 for his $10 billion Murray-Darling management plan, with critics claiming the amount of spending was determined not by necessity but by the goal of seeking maximum attention for the announcement. Yet today this trend is common, as proponents signal the importance of an issue and their eagerness to garner public support for it by dedicating a great amount of money to it.

Julia Gillard never escaped her on-camera commitment to 'no carbon tax under the government I lead' prior to the 2010 election, despite the reality of a hung parliament that required her, in order to form government, to negotiate with others for whom such a policy was in fact a priority.

The election-eve interview Tony Abbott gave on the relatively low-rating SBS where he promised 'No cuts to education, no cuts to health, no change to pensions, no change to the GST and no cuts to the ABC or SBS' came back to politically haunt the government after the 2014 budget, despite it having a much stronger parliamentary position than Gillard had had.

The pursuit of simplicity in messaging, which is often a result of the behaviour of the mass media and the techniques and demands of social media, has made the public endorsement and enaction of complex initiatives—from climate change policy to balancing the budget—much harder to achieve than it needs to be.

PARTIES THAT SEEK TO GOVERN

The challenges described above are having a big impact on one of the most important yet under-rated institutions in politics—the parties. I say this because, despite regular disparagement, the importance of strong, well-functioning political parties is critical to a transparent, successful democracy.

We don't have to imagine what it is like without them. We just need to turn to history. In many colonies prior to the rise of the two-party system, governments rose and fell without elections. They found themselves constantly horse-trading for survival and the passage of legislation, and opportunities for cronyism and favouritism abounded. The truth is that political parties play a critical role in bringing together people with shared values to form coherent policy platforms, which are then offered to citizens who can consider them at an election.

Political parties are the mechanism by which we develop coherent policy agendas that have a strong chance of electoral endorsement, and which are worthy of being put before parliament for implementation. Such agendas require trade-offs and compromises across the enormous spectrum of individual views that exist in society, and these are achieved within parties. The alternative would be sundry policies put before the electorate by individual candidates, which effectively places them beyond a democratic choice, as they would all need to be negotiated post election when leaders seek to gather support to form a government.

Furthermore, while public commentary often criticises what's called 'party discipline' as constraining the freedom of politicians to express their personal views, the very existence of such discipline ensures accountability. Members of a government elected on a party platform are held accountable for its implementation. If all of us were independents, unbound by a coherent agenda, the notion of liability increasingly would be tested through the amount of public funds directed locally, turning politics into a cargo cult of electoral bribes absent common or national interest. The path of American congressional politics is not one to aspire to.

Yet while parties are critical institutions, they are weakened ones.

The memberships of political parties are a fraction of what they were two generations ago, and they continue to fall. Both major parties in Australia have well under 100 000 members—this across a nation of nearly seventeen million voters. At the same time, community engagement with single-issue or specific-campaign movements is growing. Whether it's an organised and openly electoral and political campaigning body, such as GetUp!, or a movement expressed through more direct public participation, such as the BLM protest marches of 2020, individual causes or perspectives that explicitly avoid a wide-ranging platform are succeeding, not failing, in attracting support. In essence, movements that don't require the sentiments of compromise or prioritisation are strengthening at the expense of political parties which need to do so in order to viably govern.

This has led to the growing power of the fringe, which is primarily expressed in two forms: first, as parties that aim not to form government but to influence it; and second, as single-issue groups that similarly do not seek elected office but rather to influence it—sometimes by agitating for higher priority to be given to an issue, and sometimes by looking to veto the consideration of a less-favoured policy.

Significantly, by not seeking to form government, these actors are avoiding the single, most important activity major political parties and governments undertake: prioritisation and trade-offs in regard to competing demands on public resources. For in a debate between interest groups, every issue can have equal billing, an equal claim to priority. There is seemingly no limit on the public resources that can be allocated. This imaginary world is used against the political parties that have to do the exact opposite: govern by implementing programs that do add up, minus any fanciful claims of giving everyone everything they want.

The Overton window is a term that has frequently been used in recent years. In short, it refers to how politicians and other electoral players choose policies that are within the realm of public acceptability to maximise their chances of success. For someone seeking office, proposing policy that lies outside this window of public acceptance risks being counterproductive, in that they will not win office and therefore cannot implement their preferred agenda. However, the window isn't fixed or static. Politics is effectively 'downstream' of the broader society and culture, and as values and norms change, so does what is politically acceptable—that is, the Overton window can shift, and it can widen to encompass evolving or new views. As an example, the White Australia immigration regime was broadly supported a century ago, but race-based immigration policy is considered unacceptable now.

The point here is that, while major political parties, those who seek to govern, operate broadly within such a constraint, fringe or minor parties and single-issue groups do not. Indeed, they have a different incentive—to move the window or change it, rather than seek electoral success within it. This can be quite healthy, such as in the efforts to transform what is acceptable in terms of immigration and race, which have indeed dramatically changed in my own lifetime. Where it is not healthy is where it attempts to conduct some sort of litmus test on a political party or policy item.

More and more, the new media world facilitates and encourages this. Whether reflecting the views and perspectives of groups drawn from narrower social groups, or comprising a strategy to generate subscriptions, viewers or readers, increasingly, those within major parties hear assertions that a particular policy or position is absolutely necessary to reflect a party's constituency.

THE MINOR PARTIES

Modern minor parties have very different incentives to those of the parties intent on governing. They may advocate a particular policy agenda, or they may seek patronage and preferment in the allocation of public resources, or sometimes they aim for a combination of both. But a key aspect of minor parties, especially the newer incarnations, is who they see as their prime electoral competition.

Historically, if a minor party was a breakaway from a major party, it often explicitly campaigned against that major party; for example, the Democratic Labour Party from the 1950s through the 1970s. At other times, it represented a defined sectional interest, such as with the formation of the Country Party in 1920.

The Australian Democrats, the most prominent minor party of the previous generation, and until recently the most successful, had a different agenda, partly expressed so bluntly in inaugural leader Don Chipp's famous words, 'Keep the bastards honest.' Following on from the short-lived Australia Party, it was explicitly middle-of-the-road, with the aim of negotiating with both sides of politics. It was also a party set up in the spirit of facilitating compromise within the parliamentary process, specifically in the Senate.

Whether working with Paul Keating on native title, Peter Reith on workplace relations, or, eventually, John Howard on the GST, the Australian Democrats saw their role as broadly accepting a mandate but ameliorating specific policy concerns. However, the party's last successful compromise, on the GST, was a harbinger of the new politics to come. Not only was conciliation no longer the path to electoral success, it was to trigger the collapse of the party as its electoral base abandoned it, partly for a replacement that overtly spurned compromise.

The Greens, now Australia's largest minor party, is a very different party to the Australian Democrats. The rise of The Greens as a national force shines a light on the trends outlined above: the demonisation of compromise; a specific ideological agenda; a lack of interest in cooperating with a governing majority, or respecting its electoral mandate. The language used by The Greens is instead often absolute and moralistic; for example, the claim that Australia's immigration policies are responsible for people dying.

Even more notably, it has been entirely open about competing with the Labor Party for progressive voters. The seats it has won in parliament have more often than not come at the expense of traditional Labor seats, albeit alongside substantial demographic change. The parliamentary tactics of The Greens are also often directed at differentiating the party from Labor on issues where both major parties agree. 'Wedge politics' is the apt term that describes how The Greens positions itself against the Labor Party on issues where Labor is vulnerable to being seen to compromise for electoral viability—such as on immigration policy—to a targeted cohort of progressive voters.

Similarly, One Nation often tries to position itself in opposition to the Coalition, and particularly the National Party, knowing that its appeal to those parties' supporters is a major component of its success. In opposing policies to address climate change, and attacking banks, and supporting rural protectionist measures, it sees its prime electoral competition as being the Coalition.

Looking at the social media activity of the minor parties, you often see emotive, simplistic claims that are critical of 'both major parties' (that is, those who seek government). Occasionally impugning motives (they are 'in the pocket of big business'), the messages do not encourage people to weigh up a competing agenda but rather to dismiss it and those proposing it. This represents a move away from the utilitarianism of seeking agreement in the common interest, as more minor parties seek patronage for their constituencies. Whether it's Nick Xenophon and his heirs seeking benefits for South Australia, or Brian Harradine and Jacqui Lambie seeking similar for Tasmania, the new minor parties have put special claims above common ones. Similarly, while not geographically defined, The Greens reinforces this approach.

The greater issue is that the minor parties campaign against those who want to govern. Government can only be delivered by one of the major parties, even if in a coalition or other arrangement with minor parties. So the motivation here is merely to target part of the electorate, whether geographic or demographic, and thereby attain power over government rather than within it. The strategy is to criticise the necessary compromises required of parties that are trying to build a broad base of support to underpin a government, to bypass the scrutiny of the media and target voters' grievances.

Why is this challenge to the main political parties so significant? Because other than voters, they are the critical actors in the political system. They define politics, as voters must effectively choose from among them for government. The increase in elections of independents in recent decades is notable, as these usually reflect local concerns and, more often than not, have occurred in more easily defined electoral communities outside capital cities. But while independents can assist in forming a government—although their record of success in recent times has been patchy—they cannot form it themselves.

CLOSE ELECTIONS

One final element that makes compromise more difficult, and which has been especially noted in the United States in recent years, is the impact of close elections. In short, where electoral contests are more regularly very close, and therefore the potential for changes in those who hold offices of power or government are more regular, there is an incentive to maintain a position and wait for a future opportunity to implement more of one's mandate, or to keep an issue at the forefront of the political agenda.

The United States highlights how refusing to allow those in office to claim 'victory' on an issue by virtue of its resolution—for example, on gaining passage for legislation—denies them the credit for its settlement. Similarly, the ability to frustrate a government by preventing it from addressing an issue of public concern causes greater political problems for that government than it does for the opposition. In the words of the political commentator Ezra Klein, 'Compromise isn't a gift the majority offers to a minority. It's a boon the minority offers to the majority.'

As outlined at the beginning of this book, Australia has recently seen its closest electoral results at the federal level in decades. Political incentives have now changed—the potential to frustrate a government and cause negative sentiment towards those in office when electoral margins are so narrow can outweigh the desire to resolve a public issue, particularly when minor parties are focused on seeking electoral success through grievance or the demonisation of compromise.

FUTURE CHALLENGES

The concerns I have described present a major challenge to Australian politics in a number of ways.

First, there is the well-noted declining trust in politics and institutions, which is widely expressed in surveys and the tone of public debates. If this continues, it will only make the trends outlined above even more problematic. In the end, our political system is the only means by which to address issues collectively.

Second, we are already beginning to see the rise of so-called alternatives to the traditional electoral and political process. The most prominent example of these is the so-called 'citizen jury'. Citizen juries are comprised of a representative selection of individuals who are presented with a policy challenge, selected experts and evidence, and who then deliberate the issue before arriving at an outcome. Underpinning this approach is a scepticism that is directed at the way in which modern democracy tackles complex policy problems.

The newDemocracy Foundation is a leading proponent of citizen juries in Australia. On the principle of random selection, the foundation states on its website that

> [g]overnments inevitably hear from the noisiest voices who insist on being heard.

In contrast, society trusts 12 randomly-selected people on a criminal jury to assess evidence, discuss their views and reach a consensus recommendation because random selection generates 'people like us'. Our process gets beyond the enraged and the articulate because the public would perceive them as having a bias.

Such processes have garnered supporters precisely because of a perceived failure of politics in addressing big problems. But the inevitable consequence is that democracy, as exemplified in the debate and determination by electoral processes and representatives, is demeaned.

Furthermore, the inherent lack of direct engagement with the great mass of citizens through the electoral process creates a significant issue of legitimacy and consent. While this and similar approaches are used dealing with smaller, technical or less contentious issues, and may prove valuable in guiding administrators on how to best implement a solution, as soon as they deal with a highly divisive issue, the aforementioned problems will apply in an even stronger fashion. Without any way of having a direct say over those making decisions, or the ability to dismiss those appointed to do so, then impugning the motives of those participating or even managing the process could very easily poison any outcome.

It is often written that in the 1980s and 1990s, Australia handled the extraordinarily complex policy challenge of reforming an historically protected economy while ensuring that economic inequality did not open up as it had in the United States or the United Kingdom. This was undertaken with both sides of politics occasionally agreeing but often contesting policy proposals. There was broad agreement on economic issues such as trade liberalisation and financial market deregulation, but disagreement on elements like Medicare and the GST. However, it was a combination of electoral contests and negotiation and compromise that delivered the end result.

This combination will be just as critical when Australia deals with new challenges. The last decade alone has illustrated that tackling the social and economic consequences of climate change, emissions reductions and economic reform is an extremely complicated matter, lying well beyond a single electoral contest. And at this point, we cannot truly contemplate the longer-term effects of the COVID-19 pandemic across society, let alone the global effects that will directly impact Australia.

What we do know is that different voices and experiences need to be heard and acknowledged, ensuring a plurality of viewpoints and thereby making any outcome more enduring. In order to address one challenge and move on to the next one, there must be a dynamic and effective sense of compromise.

WHAT CAN WE DO ABOUT THIS?

The challenges are always easier to outline than the solutions—at least, this is true of every serious issue. But here are some suggestions.

One possible answer is institutional, building on the now traditional role of the Senate as a key forum for compromise on nationally contentious policy. It shouldn't surprise anyone that, as a senator, I suggest something along those lines. And I do so because, if one looks at national policy achievements in recent decades, electoral contests and debates have seen their resolution through negotiation in the Senate.

One of the fears of those who are on the side of electoral defeat is that compromise on an issue entails giving up on one's priorities—that a new status quo is then established that becomes impossible to overturn or reconsider. I have always held the view that the reconsideration of issues that I have thought are settled in favour of my world view does not represent a risk, but rather an opportunity to further engage the public in seeking support for them.

One tool not widely used in Australia, but which has occasionally been applied to national security legislation, is the 'sunset clause'. In essence, this means that legislation either expires in its legal effect, or it requires reconsideration after a certain period of time before a further regulation takes effect or another policy step is taken. It is often used in the context that a review of the impact of a law or policy has been mandated, but it rarely freezes the operation of a law pending a review by parliament.

Now in some areas, this approach may not deliver the desired long-term certainty, such as where substantial investment is involved. However, that is not always the case. Where measures involve the imposition of regulatory burdens or costs on some for the benefit of others, it may lead to the easier settlement of an issue, with the knowledge that such a cost will not be imposed without future reconsideration. It is suited to other areas, too, such as where long-term increases in mandated government spending are legislated.

A sunset clause ensures that issues are revisited by parliament, with the views of all in the community again represented at a future time. When it comes to prioritising limited resources, this should be seen as an opportunity, one that would require consideration not merely from those in government at the time, and not starting simply from the status quo. For example, with the myriad welfare and transfer payments that have developed over time, surely forcing a parliamentary reassessment of the social security system from first principles, and through the prism of the world today, would not be harmful.

Maybe people are right to be cynical about this proposal from a politician who has directly participated in this environment for more than a decade. In fact, some scepticism is appropriate. I am not going to claim I haven't occasionally been guilty of some of the tendencies I have outlined. People shouldn't seek perfection in politics or politicians, as to expect such will only lead to disappointment.

That said, politicians can reflect as well, and the best way to illustrate the need to compromise is to demonstrate that it works. In politics, saying no to one's opponents is easy, and saying yes to your own supporters is easy as well. True leadership rests in challenging the electorate, particularly those whom you are closest to. When John Howard and Tim Fischer demanded radical, national gun law reform in the aftermath of the Port Arthur massacre in April 1996, it was much more challenging to communities represented by the Coalition.

On a personal level, this is also the responsibility of each member of parliament. No-one can assert that every policy pursued by their own side is one they agree with or think is a priority. Every member or senator will at some point be called upon to support something they do not personally favour. Often, this is portrayed in the media as 'toeing the party line', or a sign of weakness in the individual for not standing up for their own views. But I say it can be regarded as a willingness to work with others, a willingness to be practical, to compromise.

When a debate over difficult issues comes before parliament, those who express different views within a party are often asked whether they will 'cross the floor' to make clear their opposition. I have confronted this often. In 2014, for instance, I didn't like some aspects of that year's budget, specifically the income tax surcharge. But being a member of the ministry, I was bound to support it, and I did so without any real internal conflict. Budgets, by their nature, are put together by a handful of senior ministers balancing many competing needs. To have members of government pick and choose from among measures would lead to chaos.

More recently, I was personally troubled by some aspects of the higher education changes legislated in late 2020, in particular the impact on the humanities area, and on students finishing high school that year. I discussed these at length with the education minister, but it was clear that my concerns were echoed only by a small minority within the government. Should I have crossed the floor to bring down the proposals in the Senate? That's the populist view. But a more serious understanding invites the question of whether it really would be appropriate for a single senator in the government to block a comprehensive policy that has been through a deliberative Cabinet process, followed by party-wide consideration. For those who say this was about career progression, that didn't apply in my case as I had already announced my retirement at the next election. It was actually about a sense of humility—the recognition that, on an issue that can always be reconsidered in the future (higher education has regularly been re-evaluated over the past two decades), it shouldn't be my point of view alone that determines the passage of the changes.

The use of compromise as a source of progress can also be illustrated by something that is likely to be a focus of public debate for some time: the recognition of Aboriginal and Torres Strait Islander people in the Australian Constitution.

I have long opposed the notion of further entrenching race in our constitution. I see the use of race as something in our history that we need to be brutally honest about, and critical of. As a liberal, I see the most recent decade as having moved away from holding up race as any sort of defining concept of a fellow citizen, and that this is something that should continue. That said, I accept that there are different perspectives on this, even if I disagree with some of them, including an embrace of the concept of Indigenous peoples rather than race—the idea that Indigenous peoples have a different, special claim to their standing that other communities do not have. Also, opposition to such a constitutional measure isn't meant to deny the fact that Indigenous Australians were long formally denied the basic rights of citizenship and suffered an extraordinary disadvantage that remains a tragedy today.

Without getting into arguments about practical versus symbolic reconciliation, I am not alone in this. There are a significant number of people who are troubled by the notion of a race-based body being inserted into our constitution. Those of us with an awareness of the history of referenda would also not like to see such a measure put to the people only to fail, for it is certain there will be a 'no' case. Yet if the aspiration is to ensure a greater Indigenous voice in policymaking, should that worthwhile objective fall down on this constitutional proposal?

Indeed, Ken Wyatt, the Minister for Indigenous Australia, has proposed the legislation of new models of local decision-making to provide a body that represents an 'Indigenous voice to government'. This will require compromise from those of us concerned about the role of race in such measures. And for others aspiring to a constitutional measure, I hope it also represents a step forward, as it doesn't require their preferred change to be ruled out. Compromise from both sides in this case can represent progress, even if it seems imperfect to many.

We all have lines we will not cross, but in politics, whether holding or seeking government, our job is not to draw any more of them. Instead, we must find a way to deal with as many of the issues confronting modern society as possible. This requires humility on the part of politicians as well as those seeking to influence them. One's own perspective cannot be fixed in stone, or be used as the sole test for agreement.

Finally, what does all this mean for the citizens of this country? It is up to you, as much as your political representatives, to confound the challenges I've described in this book. Seek out views that you have previously not seen, heard or read. Strive to understand the perspectives and experiences of those who hold views that are different to your own. Reject those who try to impugn others when you consider political debates. And, of course, be open to the idea that compromising on a particular priority is not a failure, but rather may represent progress, if not success; that it doesn't preclude reconsideration in the future; that the perfect should not be the enemy of the good. If you do this, it will help change the incentives in politics, rewarding those who govern successfully while at the same time ensuring that those who seek the opposite are not rewarded.

The 'centre' of politics is not halfway between Liberal and Labor, or in the middle of the

Right and the Left. It represents an approach to practically addressing an important issue, even imperfectly, then moving on to the next one in the endless series of problems and other matters that politics and government must confront. The alternative is to become fixated on certain issues, never even temporarily resolving them, and have them motivate people to divide into burgeoning tribes. Do we really want our politics to be more like those of the United States, where weighty issues like abortion and gun laws are argued over for decade after decade while other concerns remain unaddressed by the political process?

The approach I'm advocating will not always mean an active state or government. For those who share my world view, it will often mean arguing the case that the proposed government action is not warranted, that it will create other problems or even compound the one that is subject to debate. It can mean a determination not to act, or to reduce the role of government. But it will ensure that all of our voices have the opportunity to be heard, and it will give government a chance to address the multiplicity of priorities and aspirations in our enormously diverse country.

In the end, democracy is always in the hands of the citizens.

ACKNOWLEDGEMENTS

My thanks to Louise Adler, who invited me to contribute to this series and made tight time frames work so I could. Paul Smitz taught me the importance of a great editor. And I'm grateful to my colleagues across parliament, staff, officials and journalists, who tested my ideas and encouraged me to write. But thank you especially to Helen, for her endless encouragement, advice and confidence.

IN THE NATIONAL INTEREST

Other books on the issues that matter: